M000167323

A Running Press® Miniature Edition™
© 2016 by Camilla Sanderson
All rights reserved under the Pan-American and
International Copyright Conventions

Printed in China

9 8 7 6 5 4 3 2 1
Digit on the right indicates the number of this printing

Library of Congress Control Number: 2015955720

ISBN 978-0-7624-5792-2

Running Press Book Publishers
A Member of the Perseus Books Group
2300 Chestnut Street
Philadelphia, PA 19103-4371

Visit us on the web!
www.runningpress.com

Contents

What Is Mindfulness?

"Mindfulness is awareness, cultivated by paying attention in a sustained and particular way: on purpose, in the present moment, and non-judgmentally," writes Dr. Jon Kabbat-Zinn, a pioneer of mindfulness in the West.

In 1979, Kabbat-Zinn founded the Mindfulness-Based Stress Reduction (MBSR) program at the University of Massachusetts Medical School to help people with chronic pain when no other medication or treatment worked. Because of his success in a medical setting with scientifically measured results, his programs have been adapted throughout the world by medical centers, hospitals, and health maintenance organizations, in addition to schools, prisons, veteran's centers, and professional sports organizations.

Learning and practicing mindfulness meditation on a regular basis is one of the most profound gifts that we can give to ourselves. Kabbat-Zinn largely credits mindfulness as originating in Buddhism. However, mindfulness cuts through any one particular religion. We can trace its roots in many spiritual traditions, and it can be practiced by anyone from atheists, to the spiritual-but-not-religious, to the deeply religious within in any faith.

Through studying world religions for two years in interfaith seminary school, I discovered many different practices that each faith tradition offers to help people to focus their attention: from meditation to prayer; yoga to

tai'chi and qi-gong. Each religion may
have its own particular approach,
but they all offer a way to cultivate a
conscious awareness within ourselves
that facilitates a practice of mindfulness. In this sense, mindfulness can be
likened to the ability to observe our
humanity (the experience of our very
human lives) from our divinity (a kind
of benevolent, compassionate, and
empathetic observing awareness within
us). A practice of mindfulness can help
us to lessen our suffering and allows us
to transform the way we live our lives.

Meditation is one aspect of mindfulness, but mindfulness can also extend into every moment of our lives. Similar to yoga, there is no goal or destination to reach, which we are so conditioned to strive for in the West. Mindfulness is an ongoing practice that deeply enriches every aspect of our human experience, and is a practice we can cultivate for the duration of our lives.

Additionally, research in the field of stress management provides further evidence of how our thinking affects

 9

our physical bodies. This concept that our thinking affects our bodies is something that our Western medical system has continually resisted, as it's so difficult to scientifically measure and quantify. However, we can now enjoy some of the healing modalities that have worked in the East for millennia such as acupuncture, Chinese herbal medicine, and Ayurvedic medicine. Our Western medical system is slowly learning to offer what is now being called Integrative Medicine or Functional Medicine where we are treated as whole beings, including body, mind, spirit, and emotions, rather than a doctor looking only at the physical aspect of our ailment. Hence, Western medicine now recognizes the fact that cultivating a practice of mindfulness meditation is an effective tool in maintaining optimal health in body, mind, emotions, and spirit.

One of the keys of mindfulness lies in our ongoing and regular practice. Similar to brushing our teeth—if we consistently brush and floss every morning and evening, we have a better chance at preventing cavities. Likewise, if we continue to practice mindfulness meditation on a regular basis, we are practicing the art of extreme self-care. In other words, a mindfulness practice is part of the process of taking good care of our-selves on all levels: physical, mental, emotional, and spiritual. And when we take good care of ourselves, we become a breath of fresh air in our environment.

This mini book on mindfulness will provide you with a variety of seven-minute mindfulness practices, many of which you can do anywhere at any time; in addition to outlining day-to-day mindfulness ideas, concepts, and practices you can integrate into your daily life. We will consider the extensive benefits of a consistent mindfulness practice—even for just 7 minutes a day—and we'll explore what mindfulness practices look and feel like.

"Deep listening is the essence of mindfulness—a cultivating of intimacy with your own life unfolding," writes Kabbat-Zinn in *Mindfulness for Beginners*. When we become truly intimate with the unfolding of our life, we're able to step back and watch it with intense curiosity, yet remain free from attachment to outcomes. We watch ourselves experiencing both joy and pain, as we observe our blossoming and we practice mindfulness to lessen the sharpness of our suffering. We continue with the ordinary details of our lives, but the difference lies in the mindful awareness we bring to brushing our teeth, cooking our dinner, eating a meal, taking a shower.

There's a Japanese expression "Gambate kudasai" (pronounced Gam-ba-tey ku-da-sai) that we don't have an exact translation for in English, but it roughly translates to good luck, or hang in there, or keep making your best effort. And remember to have fun!

. . .

Why Practice?

The benefits of practicing mindfulness cannot be overstated. We
wouldn't consider not brushing our
teeth if we want to prevent cavities.
How can we consider not cultivating
a practice that so deeply nourishes
our well-being?

Historically, religions offered care
for our spiritual well-being; however,
with the crumbling patriarchal hierarchies, dogma, and regulations that

exist in so many organized religions, people now look for other ways to care for our spiritual natures. Yet it would be foolish to dismiss the spiritual wisdom of the ages that exists throughout all faith traditions.

From Hinduism, the world's *oldest religion* (and third largest; Christianity being the largest, and Islam second) to Shamanism, the world's *oldest indigenous spiritual practice* (rivaled perhaps by the Australian Aboriginal *Dreamtime*) to Judaism, Buddhism, Taoism, Sikhism, and more, each and every faith tradition offers deep wisdom. However, as religions no longer seem to serve so many of us, we need to maintain a sense of our spiritual nature by cultivating our own rituals and practices that will honor the sacred within. One way to do this is to develop a practice of mindfulness meditation.

Even if a person may be a devout follower of a particular religion, mindfulness meditation can encourage a Jew to dive deeper into Judaism, a Christian to further explore

Christianity—perhaps exploring the work of the Christian Mystics of the ages, or learning *Centering Prayer* as discussed in Father Thomas Keating's *Open Mind, Open Heart*. Mindfulness meditation is a practice that cuts through any spiritual tradition we may identify with, and facilitates a deeper practice in any faith.

Furthermore, a person may be an atheist and/or a Humanist and have no belief in a spiritual realm whatsoever, and yet mindfulness meditation can also serve them well.

The benefits of mindfulness meditation can include:

Lowering stress: This has been well documented by Kabat-Zinn's extensive work in Mindfulness Based Stress Reduction (MBSR).

Managing pain: Again, Kabat-Zinn's work provides scientific evidence of great success.

Lowering reactivity: By cultivating the awareness behind our thinking, we slowly begin to realize that we are not our thoughts. When we're no longer identified with our thoughts, we have more space around how we respond to different people and situations; hence we may not be as quick to anger or react in haste.

Increasing compassion: By getting to know and accept our own thoughts, we slowly move towards radical self-acceptance, and as we have more love and compassion for ourselves, we can extend the same to others.

 21

Decreasing negative thought chatter and anxiety: As we increase our capacity to observe our own thoughts, when any negative thought chatter begins, we have a chance to detach from that negative chatter and observe it, rather than being identified with it and getting beaten down.

Facilitating the dance of will and surrender: In our Western culture, we love to feel that we are in control. And we do have control over many elements in our lives; however, not all. When we experience a crisis, especially in love, money, or health, we gain the experience of not being in control, and usually we suffer. But if we cultivate mindfulness meditation, we facilitate our surrender to what is. By surrendering to the present moment and the reality of the situation, we help alleviate much of our suffering.

Neuroplasticity: Sustained meditation leads to neuroplasticity, which is defined as the brain's ability to change, structurally and functionally, on the basis of environmental input. For much of the last century, scientists believed that the brain essentially stopped changing after adulthood, but we now know this is false, and mindfulness meditation is healthy exercise for our brains.

Keeps our brains healthy: Studies have shown that people who meditate have thicker cortical walls than non-meditators. This means that their brains age at a slower rate. Cortical thickness is also associated with decision making, attention, and memory.

Physical benefits: Improved sleep and lowered blood pressure.

A simple Google search on the benefits of mindfulness meditation will uncover even more of the diverse and plentiful benefits of mindfulness meditation. The real question is why *wouldn't* we practice?

And if your response is that you don't have enough time, there is an

old Zen proverb: "Sitting in meditation for twenty minutes every
day will benefit you greatly—unless
you're too busy. Then you need to sit
for an hour."

Part One

7-MINUTE PRACTICES OF MINDFULNESS MEDITATION

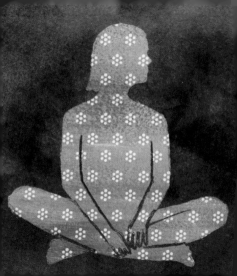

7-Minute Sitting Practice

Have you ever paused to consider who is breathing you? We continue to breathe, even when we're not consciously trying to. It's kind of miraculous when you stop to consider it.

This practice can be done anywhere, at any time of day. If you're at work, just close your door, or find a meeting room where you can sit undisturbed for seven minutes. Or if it's a nice day outside, is there a park you can sit in where you'll feel okay about sitting with your eyes closed? It's possible to put cell phone ear plugs in your ears to pretend you're listening to music. If you're at home, find a comfortable place to sit. Try to ensure you won't be disturbed.

If you have your cell phone you can set the timer for 7 minutes. Otherwise, you'll need some other kind of timer.

Sit in a way that you feel relaxed and upright, in a firm but not stiff position. With your eyes closed, your feet either on the ground or sitting in a cross-legged position, your back aligned with your neck, your chin slightly down, which will bring the crown of your head up high and stretch your spine up, and your hands resting in your lap; bring your awareness to your breathing. Breathing through your nose, notice your breath coming in and nourishing your body with oxygen. Don't force your breathing. Simply observe the deep inhale and the following exhale. Comfortable clothes work well for this practice, or you may want to open a button on your pants.

Continue to observe your breath, inhaling and exhaling. At some point you'll notice that your thoughts have drifted somewhere else. As soon as you notice your thoughts are elsewhere, with kindness and compassion, bring your awareness back to your breath. "Oh, my thoughts have drifted; I'm bringing my attention back to my breath." Rinse and repeat—I wrote that to make you smile. But truly, that's all mindfulness meditation is—a practice of continually bringing your awareness back to the present moment.

It's important to remember that *there is no failure* with any kind of meditation. This practice is simply a process of continually bringing your awareness back to your breath. A good analogy is when we train a puppy to pee on a mat—we don't want to be mean to the puppy, we just want to continually bring it back to the mat, and give it lots of love and encouragement. We want to bring our awareness back to the present moment in the same way.

You will benefit from only 7 minutes of this sitting meditation practice, but you'll notice even greater benefit with 20 minutes a day. In either case, 7 minutes a day is better than an hour once a month. Mindfulness is best practiced daily.

"You are the sky; everything else is just the weather."

—Pemma Chodron

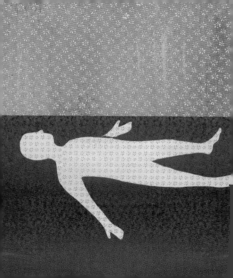

7-Minute Body Scanning Practice

Have you ever considered the idea: We are not our body; we're the soul that resides in our body?

This is a restful and rejuvenating practice for our bodies.

You'll need a place where you can lie down for 7 minutes, undisturbed. I've even had co-workers lie down under their desks to do this practice. Again, you can set your timer for 7 minutes.

When you're lying down on your back in a comfortable place, where you're not too warm or too cool (sometimes it's nice to have a blanket over you), close your eyes and begin to scan your body. Begin with bringing your awareness to your left big toe. Slowly bring your awareness to the next toe, then each other toe. Bring your awareness to the arch of your left foot, to your heel, to your ankle. Imagine breathing into your left foot. Slowly travel up your left leg, feeling into and sensing each part—your calves, shins, knees, thighs. When you get to your pelvis, bring your attention to the big toe of the right foot, and slowly breathe into each part of your right foot and leg, slowly reaching back up to the pelvis.

Bring your awareness to the solar plexus (which is a couple of finger widths below your belly button) then to your waist, your back touching the floor, your chest. See if you can sense into your lungs inside your chest, your heart, and up to your shoulders.

Bring your attention to both of your hands, each of your fingers, and wrists. Slowly sense into each area of your lower arms, then upper arms, returning to the shoulders. Now up through your neck and throat, sense every part of your face, the back of your head, and end with the crown of your head.

Imagine breathing in through a hole in the top of your head, allowing energy to reach all the way down to the tips of your toes, breathing out through your toes, then back in through your toes and the energy traveling back up to and out of the crown of your head with your exhale. Continue this flow of breathing in through the top of your head, through your body, out through your toes, back in through your toes and up through your body to back out through the crown of your head. Continue this breathing until your timer beeps or until you feel rested and rejuvenated. It can feel as though our body drops away and all we're conscious of is flowing breath. We can allow that feeling of being more than our body. You can also practice feeling into the deep stillness within your heart.

As you finish this practice, bring your awareness back to your whole physical body. Wiggle your toes and fingers and start to slowly roll your limbs side to side. You can also begin to observe your surroundings as you bring yourself back into your physical being in the world feeling refreshed and rejuvenated.

7-Minute Walking Practice

Do you need a break from working at your desk? Or perhaps you simply have some time to get up and go for a mindfulness walk. Whatever opportunity presents itself, seize it, and begin.

Start with this warming-up practice: stand with your two feet about hip-distance apart. Bend your knees slightly, and bring your attention to

your dan tien—your energy center—which is about two or three finger's width below your belly button, and right in the center of the width of your body.

Now bring your focus to your lower abdomen and engage your muscles, which will tilt your pelvis slightly upwards at the front of your body. Think of your pelvis as a wok or a shallow bowl, and you want it to be level, so the energy doesn't tip out. Play with the feeling of tilting your pelvis back and forth, so you get an understanding and body awareness of keeping it level with your lower stomach muscles engaged.

Standing with your knees slightly bent, lower abs engaged, pelvis level, and your awareness in your dan tien; this is your grounding stance. You can bring your arms up and circle them in front of your chest as though you were hugging a big, round ball. Breathe into this grounding stance for a few breaths.

Drop your arms when you're ready to begin walking. Look straight ahead, not at your feet. Keep your lower abs engaged with your pelvis level, and continue bringing your awareness to your dan tien. As you walk, imagine a needle going up through your pelvis, through your spine, and out the crown of your head with your chin slightly lowered. Be aware of how your pelvis rotates around the pin as you walk.

As is the same with all meditation and mindfulness practices, *there is no failure!* And at some point you will notice that your thoughts have begun to wander. Say to yourself with kindness and compassion, "Oh, my thoughts have wandered, I'm bringing my attention back to my dan tien and to the present moment."

You may simply walk in circles in a room, or if you're going to walk outside, have the route already planned out, so there is no need to think of anything else as you are walking. Sometimes it's useful to practice walking meditation very slowly, to facilitate bringing our awareness back to our dan tien, but feel free to walk at any pace that feels right to you.

You may continue walking for at least 7 minutes, or for as long as you feel a need.

If you are interested in developing this practice further, I invite you to explore *ChiRunning* (and *ChiWalking*) by Danny Dryer.

7-Minute Practice of the Dance of Will and Surrender

Our Western culture encourages us to develop our *will* and a sense of control. Make it happen, get it done, you can do it! Encouraging us to think we're in complete control of our lives. It's often only once we've experienced a major crisis in love, money, or health that we begin to understand how little control we truly have. But if you haven't expe-

rienced such a crisis, take a moment
to consider what you don't control in
your life. Life can change in an instant.

Once we understand we're not
completely in control, we can begin
to consider the *surrender* part of the
dance. We can practice surrendering
to a higher power. Trusting in the
universe. There can be enormous
freedom, liberation, relief, relaxation,
and joyful ecstasy with surrender.

You can practice surrender with
sitting mindfulness meditation: set
your timer, follow the sitting mind-

fulness meditation instructions (see p.29), and begin with your awareness in your heart while using the word *surrender* as a mantra—repeating it to yourself as you breathe in and out, surrendering into the peaceful stillness deep within your heart.

Every time you notice your attention has wandered, with compassion and kindness, repeat the word *surrender* and bring your awareness back to the peaceful quiet within your heart as you breathe in and breathe out. Continue for a 7-minute mindfulness surrender practice.

When we practice a surrender mindfulness meditation, we drop into the Flow of Life. We have a feeling of being in our body as a spiritual being having a human experience; watching depth and beauty unfolding in both the joy and the pain we experience in our humanity. By cultivating surrender as part of our mindfulness practice with a continual bringing of our awareness back to the deep stillness in our heart, we tap into Divine Love.

Surrender has nothing to do with

 54

passivity. We learn that right actions do get shown. And when right actions are revealed, we use our will and take assertive action. We move back into the *will* part of the dance.

It's a shift in thinking. We learn to understand that we're not in control of everything in our life, and we learn to surrender to Life; to the deep, internal peace within our hearts; to a higher power.

I invite you to explore this concept further with Tosha Silver's book: *Outrageous Openness: Letting the Divine Take the Lead.*

"Surrender is essential to delight in, say, the bliss of orgasm, or a belly laugh, or to drift off to sleep."

—The Ecstasy of Surrender,
Judith Orloff MD

7-Minute Practice of an Attitude of Gratitude

This practice never fails to make me feel happy. When I stop and count my blessings, when I get out of bed in the morning and think "thank you" as my feet touch the floor, when I walk out my front door and deeply inhale the fresh air, when I look up into the stars at night, when my husband and partner-in-life cuddles

me, when I feel the warmth of my little kitty lean into me . . . each moment represents something to feel gratitude for.

Stop what you're doing, set a timer for seven minutes, grab a paper and pencil, or a word processing program you use, and brainstorm everything you feel grateful for. From the smell of coffee in the morning, to your blood circulating through your body, to having a healthy body, to appreciating your most heartfelt friendships, to having love in your life—love shared with a partner, a pet, a child, or simply having the feeling of impersonal love—love for the planet and our fellow spiritual beings having a human experience; to sitting there, reading these words and feeling grateful for this mini book on mindfulness reminding you to cultivate gratitude. Don't limit yourself. Go nuts for a full seven minutes. Then keep that list, and revisit it frequently to bring your awareness into the present moment. Be in your body, and feel gratitude for what is, right now.

Like I said, this practice never fails to make me feel happy, and it can be done anytime, anywhere.

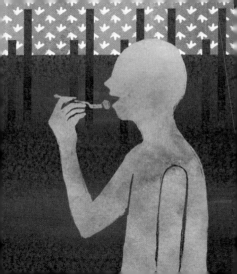

7-Minute Mindful Eating Practice

Of course the healthiest kind of mindful eating is when we're feeding ourselves nourishing and nutritious foods that we're eating in a very present and aware fashion. But this doesn't always happen. Sometimes we just grab whatever we can find to eat and wolf it down, often without even being conscious of what we're eating.

To practice mindfulness while eating, try this Buddhist mindfulness practice of eating one raisin and imagining you've never seen or tasted anything like it before. Hold it in your hand, and notice the size, color, shape, weight, texture. Take about 7 minutes to use every single one of your senses; what does it look like in detail—how would you describe it to someone who is blind and has never seen a raisin? How does it sound if you squish it between your thumb and fingers near your ear? Does it have a smell if you rip it open? How does it feel to touch it—what words can you use to describe its texture? What are all the ways you can appreciate then eat that divine raisin? Get creative—tap into your right brain and notice things about the raisin that you've never noticed about a raisin before. When you go to eat it, just take a tiny bite out of it and roll it around your mouth as you chew, savoring it as much as possible, while continually bringing your attention back to how to appreciate the raisin.

Play with this practice and have fun with it.

Mindful eating is a great practice that can be extended to even just one bite of any meal you eat.

Furthermore, if you pay attention to where and how your food is grown, harvested, and prepared, you will notice that the more mindful way this is done, the more vital the food is. Practices like organic and bio-dynamic farming recognize and benefit from this kind of mindfulness. My husband has even commented that a meal "was singing" when it had been created with local and organic food, and was prepared in a mindful and conscious fashion.

As Michael Pollan recently said in an interview with Oprah, "Our most profound engagement with the natural world happens on our plates . . . Three times a day we get to express our values through food . . . Where does your food come from? You have the opportunity to support local in a very real way. That's very empowering!"

One thing to note though, if you make the choice to eat something that doesn't fall into the category of nourishing and nutritious, be *extra* mindful when you're eating it, and pay extra attention to how much you are enjoying that chocolate (for example). No matter what the food is, your *attitude* about that food matters. If you feel bad or guilty about eating that food, this in itself will have a negative effect on your body.

Relish every bite, every chew, the feel of it in your mouth, the taste of each morsel, how it feels on your tongue, the color, the texture, can you smell it? Practice deriving the maximum pleasure possible from the treat you've chosen to give to yourself.

Absolutely do not give yourself a hard time about eating the chocolate once you have made the decision that you are going to eat it. If you've chosen to eat the chocolate, revel in the chocolate. This way you're not stressing your body by feeling guilty or bad about eating something that you don't think is healthy for you.

Sometimes the way we stress our-selves out if we think we're making a "bad" choice can be worse for our bodies than the actual thing we're eating.

7-Minute (or Less) Waiting Practice

Being an inherently impatient person, when I read about this practice, it was as though a light bulb went on. What better opportunity to practice mindfulness for *any* amount of time, than when we're waiting—for anything. For example, waiting for the computer to load up, the software program to shut down, while we're waiting in line, sitting in traffic.

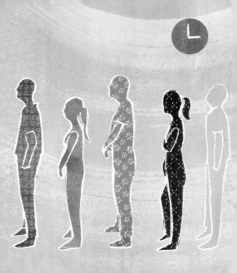

Take the opportunity to bring your attention to your breath, and do a mini mindfulness practice. Be fully here in this present moment right now, breathing in and breathing out. Simply experiencing the moment, without feeling impatient for the next event to occur. Believe me, I know this is easy to write about, but it takes a lifetime to put it into practice.

The beauty of this practice is the multitude of opportunities we get to work it seamlessly into our day-to-day life, and as we cultivate yet another daily mindfulness practice, we enjoy reaping the profound benefits to our bodies, minds, emotions, and spirits over the duration of our entire lives.

Part Two

SUSTAINING PRACTICES

Holding our Ego Like a Beloved Pet, and Laughing at It when It Tries to Run the Show

One of the greatest benefits of mindfulness meditation is becoming aware of, and gaining a separation from our ego. We learn that we are not our ego. Our egos can be very useful and serve our confidence and chutzpah in living in the world. But if we're identified with our ego, it can cause us immense suffering.

One way to investigate if our ego is running the show is to notice if we feel either inferior or superior to another person. As Eckhart Tolle says: "Whenever you feel superior or inferior to anyone, that's the ego in you."

A fun practice is to try to catch yourself in a moment when your ego is in charge. It's most often when we're in our head and not our heart, and we may be feeling a little anxious or nervous . . . When we notice our ego is engaged, we can remind ourselves: "Blessed are we who can laugh at ourselves, as we shall be endlessly amused."

In any particular moment, to practice getting separation from our ego and moving into our heart and intuition, or more in-tune with our soul, an easy physical movement we can make is to put our hand over our heart, and speak as though we're speaking from our heart. This simple physical movement will shift our energy to a place of mindful awareness immediately.

Another way to identify our ego, and to keep a healthy separation, is to practice envisioning it as a beloved pet—for example, a little pug dog called Oscar. Giving it physical attributes and a name can help us identify with amusement when we're operating from our ego. It's fun to catch Oscar when he thinks he's in charge, and to joyfully laugh at little Oscar, reminding him he's a beloved pet and he's not in charge.

The ego likes us to take everything very seriously. But it doesn't allow us to have much fun. It can also be helpful to remember that often when the ego cries, the soul rejoices.

Noticing if our ego is running the show is a practice we can engage in at any time of the day. The more space we find in mindful awareness of the present moment, the more easily we can catch our ego when it sneaks in, or we can consciously choose to engage it when we need its services.

"To be mindful means to be aware. It's the energy that knows what is happening in the present moment."

— Thich Nhat Hanh,
No Mud, No Lotus

Responding Mindfully vs. Reacting

It's stressful to our psyches and to our bodies when we vehemently react to something rather than peacefully respond. When we *react,* we usually go into "fight-or-flight" mode, which increases stress in our body. If we're able to take a step back from our reaction, to not be hooked into whatever is going on, we can *respond* in a more mindful way. This will save our body a stressful reaction, in addition to allowing us to be more effective—generally we're far more effective if we're mindfully responding to a situation versus reacting in an unconscious manner.

To practice mindfully responding versus reacting, practice *observing* yourself interacting with others. Imagine climbing up out of the box and looking back in to the box, where you can observe yourself interacting in the situation, as though you were watching a character in a story.

Observe the character of "you" interacting with others, and watch as that character either reacts or responds. Over time, as you practice observing, you will notice that moment's pause before you react. In that moment, you can breathe in and breathe out, and allow a more mindful response to unfold.

For readers comfortable with spirituality, you can imagine this climbing-out-of-the-box as an opportunity to observe your humanity from your divinity—the same divinity that exists in every sentient being.

The more we practice mindfulness exercises, the better we get at employing these practices without even thinking about them, especially in times of high stress.

It serves us well to look at the practice of mindfulness as something we will continue for the duration of our lives. This is similar to concepts we learn about in yoga—it's about the journey, not the destination—especially when we stop to consider all of life is terminal, and the destination for us all is death. So let's be more mindful and enjoy the journey!

Having Fun with Mindfulness

When we stay open to the present moment, and practice being mindful of whatever is happening right now, we open ourselves up to the joy and delight in life. Even simple things like finding humor in the puns within language keep us appreciating the present moment joyfully.

When you wake up in the morning, imagine smiling into your

body. As you become conscious of breathing in, inhale smiling joyfulness deep into your body. As you put your feet on the ground, think "thank you" with each step. Take a moment to consider: *How am I going to enjoy the day? What lights me up? What can I do to practice the art of extreme self-care and have fun while doing it, so I bring a breath of fresh air to whomever I interact with?*

Take out a pen and paper and write out all the activities that light you up or bring you joy. From mindfulness walking or running to sailing, swimming, lying in the sun on the beach, writing, reading, reading to children, listening to music, playing sports, hanging out with friends, spending time in nature, preparing food with mindfulness, volunteer or service work . . . what lights you up? And how can you do at least one of those activities today, even if for just 7 minutes? By engaging in activities that light you up, you're owning and expressing the joyful energy that exists in our human experience. In a mindful way, do what makes you feel light and happy!

Authenticity vs. Perfection

I want to share a little story about being ordained an interfaith minister. I had successfully avoided all large ceremonial events up until the age of forty-seven. I avoided a high school graduation ceremony as I left school at sixteen. I was an audacious and willful teenager, and knew that I could complete what normally takes the last two years of high school—the Australian High School Certificate (H.S.C.)—in nine months at technical college when I was eighteen. What a mistake it was though, not to take the time and enjoy my last two years at school. All my life I've been in a hurry. I remember a friend from University visiting my family home one time and observing that we all had slip-on shoes.

"Don't you guys wait for each other? You wouldn't even wait for each other to tie the laces on your shoes?"

There was an element of truth to that.

In any case, after traveling and working from ages sixteen to eighteen, I completed my H.S.C. and gained entry to University. Following the same pattern, I also missed my University graduation, as I had already left for an adventure in New York City with Jamie—with whom I also managed to escape the ceremony of a wedding, as we eloped.

I had acted in various school plays, and enjoyed my role as one of the wives in our production of *The King and I*. However, the ceremonial aspects of large milestones in my life had evaded me, or I had avoided them. I didn't even want a farewell party after working for twelve years at Penguin Young Readers' Books. I resigned over the phone.

Yet, here I was, about to be ordained. I'd studied world religions for two years and completed the Tree of Life interfaith seminary program, and the next step was to be ordained in front of about a hundred people.

Everyone can relate to the human experience of feeling terrified of public speaking. I read somewhere that the fear of public speaking ranks second only to the fear of death. Why? What makes us so terrified of speaking in front of others? Is it the fear of making a fool of ourselves? Feeling reluctant to be vulnerable in front of so many people? Is it something to do with being authentic? Showing up and revealing who we really are? Allowing others to see both our gifts and our very human foibles?

And yet there is something in me that wants to get past this fear, to reach the point of being able to actually *enjoy* speaking to a group. I've had glimpses of this, and it's left me wanting more. It feels like it's one of the biggest risks I can take in my life. To be real. To show up and be authentic in front of witnesses. To dare to be in the arena. To be seen. To reveal who I really am. With all my gifts, *and* all my muck, knowing that like the lotus flower, I will blossom *because of,* not in spite of my muck. No mud, no lotus.

There were seven other women being ordained with me, and as we waited in a small room downstairs to go upstairs to the sanctuary of the Universal Unitarian church in Milford, New Hampshire, I witnessed some of my soul-sisters freaking out. "My dad is going to be out there!" one soon-to-be-Reverend said as she half-jokingly exclaimed that she needed a Valium.

As for me, I was sweating enough that I felt like it rained from my armpits. I felt relieved that I'd worn a purply-blue flowing silk scarf, allowing me to arrange it to cover the underarm sweat marks on my pale pink linen dress. Again wanting to hide what I perceived as an *imperfection*.

Just before we went upstairs to file into the main room of the church, I felt my heart beginning to beat faster. At first I simply observed these physiological reactions—sweaty armpits, racing heart. Then I questioned why we have these physiological reactions, and I thought of the science of the fight-or-flight response. Now

I'm questioning why we *choose* to put ourselves through this kind of stressful situation?

Is it so we get practice with handling this kind of stress, so that one day we'll be more excited than terrified? Is it to have friends and family witness the culmination of our two-year journey? Does it make an event more real if people we care about witness our cere-monial event? Why do we do it?

I have more questions than answers. I made it through the ordina-tion and even enjoyed some parts of it. When I got home, I posted a photo of my diploma on Facebook, and was surprised and delighted at the number of "likes" and comments. Perhaps an interfaith minister is somewhat akin to a spiritual version of the United Nations, and the idea of it appeals.

My godmother responded to my post with, "What comes next?"

"Same as before," I replied.

While my inner life had transformed, my outer life remained the same in most respects. Although one significant difference was that I'd cultivated the courage to claim my spirituality in the world, and also the courage to share my writing in the world.

I wrote to my godmother, "It was fun to have a celebration and ceremony to mark the end of a two year journey," even though it was a tad stressful too. Rev. Stephanie wisely advised us while we waited to go into the main room of the church: "It's not about perfection. It's about authenticity. *It's about authenticity and enjoying yourself.*"

This sage advice falls under the mindfulness umbrella—it's worth taking the time to contemplate authenticity versus perfection, and how our culture conditions us to strive for *perfection*, which is so often involved with feeling superior to others, and so often leads to suffering. Remember the wisdom from Eckhart Tolle—we only feel superior (or inferior) to others when we're identified with our ego, rather than staying in the awareness behind our ego. If we can be authentic and mindfully surrender to this moment *just as it is*, not as we *want* it to be, nor as our ego thinks it *should* be, we reduce our suffering considerably. This is not to say we don't want to strive for excellence—we can derive enormous satisfaction from an excellent result. It's more to do with authentically making our best effort, keeping a mindful awareness around our tricky little egos, and remaining detached from outcomes.

When does life present you with an opportunity to show up *authen-*

tically rather than *trying to be perfect* (does perfection even exist)? And what would happen if you experimented with *mindful authenticity* rather than *trying to be perfect*? Do you feel liberated and free? Do you perhaps enjoy the experience even more?

This mindfulness practice is a fun one to experiment with.

Cultivating Positive Seeds

Every moment we practice mindfulness in our lives, we are cultivating positive mindfulness seeds that grow and blossom over time. Cultivating the positive seeds rather than the negative seeds is a Buddhist concept. Vietnamese Buddhist monk Thich Nhat Hanh writes in *No Mud, No Lotus:*

"We have the seeds, the potential in us for understanding, love, compassion, and insight, as well as the seeds of anger, hate, and greed. While we can't avoid all the suffering in life, we can suffer much less by not watering the seeds of suffering inside us."

This concept is also identified in this Native American Indian wisdom story:

"A Cherokee elder was teaching his grandchildren about life.

He said to them, "A fight is going on inside me . . . it is a terrible fight between two wolves.

One wolf represents fear, anger, envy, sorrow, regret, greed, arrogance, hatefulness, unconsciousness, and lies.

The other stands for joy, peace, love, compassion, forgiveness, humility, kindness, friendliness, generosity, faith, awareness, and truth.

This same fight is going on inside of you, and inside every other person, too."

The children thought about it for a minute. Then one child asked his grandfather,

"Which wolf will win?"

The Cherokee elder replied . . .
"The one you feed."

It serves us well to mindfully cultivate all the positive seeds within our natures. That's not to disown the negative seeds—we all have those too—but our mindfulness practice resides in our choice of which seeds we cultivate.

Radical Self-Acceptance—i.e., You Don't Need Fixing

Because our cultural conditioning encourages us to strive to be *perfect*, we most often don't want to look at our darker inner realms—the shadows that we all have, and that we need to fuel our growth. Inadvertently some religions can condition us to feel bad about our very human feelings such as anger, hate, greed, lust, etc. We can mistakenly believe that these "negative seeds" are unacceptable, often making us operate in full-blown denial that we even have any negative seeds within us. But one of the most important mindfulness practices is to recognize and acknowledge *all* qualities within ourselves—the positive and the negative—*without judging* ourselves for having the negative seeds. We need to recognize and acknowledge all human beings have negative seeds—and what's empowering is that we get to make the choice to cultivate the positive not the negative. Remember Kabat-Zinn's definition: "Mindfulness is awareness, cultivated by paying attention in a sustained and particular way: on purpose, in the present moment, and non-judgmentally"— *non-judgmentally* being key.

As described in the prior section *Cultivating Positive Seeds*, a mindfulness practice encourages and cultivates the positive seeds, however, we must also treat ourselves with kindness and compassion when we recognize the negative seeds within. It's also important to remember that it is essential to engage kindness and compassion when we recognize the negative seeds in others too.

There is an enormous amount of research and plenty of books written about how we are often *so discon-nected from our own darkest inner realms* that the only way we can find those parts of ourselves, is through "projections" which occur when we subconsciously cast our shadow to the people and the world around us.

One of the keys to finding the nature of our own shadow or negative seeds, is to be aware of our judgments about others.

If we *observe* something about another person, it is not a projection. But if we *judge* it, it is a projection and a disownment of our own negative seeds or darker inner realms. Whatever we judge in others is often a reflection of the qualities that we possess but deny within ourselves. We can all know this on an intellectual level, but living it in our daily lives is another opportunity for mindfulness practice.

For example, if I get upset with someone else's selfishness/rudeness/arrogance etc. it is usually because I am having difficulty accepting these qualities within myself. So I need to look deeply within, and examine if I may have either exhibited these qualities in the past, if I may be doing so now, or I may have the capacity to demonstrate these in the future. Our planet is at a point in history when we would benefit enormously as a human race if we are able to own our own negative seeds and stop projecting our shadow onto others. We all have the capacity to cultivate profoundly positive seeds within us, in addition to observing very negative seeds within ourselves. What would happen if we practiced radical self-acceptance and choosing to cultivate our positive seeds, while accepting and owning our own negative seeds without feeding them? Could this be part of "being the change" we want to see in the world?

Simply examining our own judgments allows us to own our negative
seeds, and allows an integration to
occur. And again, we need to remind
ourselves how important it is to practice radical self-acceptance.

New York Times bestselling author
of *Minding the Body, Mending the Mind*,
Joan Borysenko, PhD writes:

"By owning our own negative or
limiting projections, we weed our
mental gardens of unkind thoughts.
The negativity we see in others is
a clue to the qualities we are afraid

to recognize in ourselves. *When you catch yourself projecting, own it by saying, "And I am that, too.""*

Practicing the art of radical self-acceptance is another mindfulness practice in our toolbox that will serve us well throughout the duration of our lives. If we observe a negative seed in ourselves and begin to judge it, we can catch our inner critic beginning a tirade with ourselves, and nip it in the bud. Through practicing radical self-acceptance we can recognize and acknowledge all of our positive *and* negative seeds; choosing to cultivate the positive seeds, and to *observe* the negative seeds with compassion and kindness. Through radical self-acceptance we also grow towards radical acceptance and impersonal love for others.

Part Three

DEEPENING PRACTICES

Impersonal Love

Our Western cultural conditioning is towards a very personal love. We may find a person who we believe has all these wonderful qualities and we may fall in love in a very personal way. Or we have a very personal love for our children, often seeing them as a reflection of ourselves.

A different kind of love is to mindfully practice impersonal love. A love for simply being alive. A love for our

human species, with our incredi-
ble gifts, powers, and abilities, in
addition to our very human flaws and
foibles. A love for the pets or animals
in our lives. A love that simply flows
unconditionally from our hearts out
into the world.

Mindfully cultivating this kind
of impersonal love serves our own
development and evolution of consciousness, in addition to serving the
same in every person we come into
contact with.

Forgiveness Practice

The Buddhist meditation practice Tonglen is about breathing in the suffering of others, and breathing out happiness, health, and success to all sentient beings. To the Western ego-engaged-mind, this can seem a little masochistic or perhaps kind of sacrificial. However, Tonglen practice really has to do with cultivating fearlessness. It's about being willing to open ourselves up to the world and a desire to be beneficial to ourselves and to others.

By being fearless and not resisting negative feelings such as being hurt, or feeling pain, we open our hearts to life. We live the full catastrophe of life, experiencing both joy and pain totally, knowing that *all* feelings are part of the human experience.

As Pema Chodron writes in *The Wisdom of No Escape:*

"The essence of the [Tonglen] practice is willingness to share pleasure and delight and the joy of life on the out-breath and willingness to feel your pain and that of others fully on the in-breath."

When we realize that the human experience is about feeling both the joy and the pain, it makes it more difficult to hold a grudge. Contemplating our fearlessness in opening our hearts to the full catastrophe of life allows us to feel compassion for others who may have intentionally or un-intentionally hurt us or caused us pain. We can practice surrendering to the experience. We can engage one of the most healing mindfulness practices both for ourselves and others; we can practice forgiveness.

This is not to say that we don't set healthy boundaries and do everything within our power to protect ourselves from harm. However, when it comes to our feelings, if we hold a grudge we're letting someone else live rent-free in our heads.

You can practice Tonglen meditation as part of a mindful forgiveness practice. But, whatever way you practice mindful forgiveness, you are giving both yourself and others a wonderful gift.

Letting Go of Worry

Whenever you begin to worry about someone, instead of sending them that negative worried energy, hold a picture of them in your mind and heart, with a loving gold light around them. See them in happiness and ease, filled with love and light, and feeling peaceful and content.

As Tosha Silver says in *Outrageous Openness: Letting the Divine Take the Lead*:

" . . . if you care about someone, worry is the worst energy you can send. It directly transmits fear and restriction since we usually visualize all the darkest possible outcomes. So even if it's well-intended, worry blankets the poor recipient's energy field in a negative energy. Imagine a black Express Mail envelope marked "Thinking of You" filled with muck, mildew, and a few skull bones.

"That's worry. So it's simple instead to learn to send blessings as soon as worry begins. Just hold the person in your mind filled with light and happiness, see them peaceful and content. Do it day after day. That's the single, most useful gift you can mentally offer anyone you love."

Many of us are attached to our worry, though. We think that we're caring about another person if we worry about them. It's such a beautiful mindfulness practice to catch yourself as soon as you begin worry, and think about sending them a healthy, healing, light and happy energy instead. What a gift you can give to the person you care about.

Another offering instead of worry is the Buddhist Metta meditation of loving kindness:

May all beings be peaceful

May all beings be happy

May all beings be safe

May all beings awaken to the light of their true nature

May all beings be free

Observing our Humanity and Finding Meaning

Memoirs are very popular these days. Cheryl Strayed's book *Wild: From Lost to Found on the Pacific Crest Trail* was made into a movie starring Reese Witherspoon, and as of this writing *Wild* has been on the *New York Times* Bestseller list for 125 weeks to date. The 2005 memoir *The Glass Castle* by Jeannette Walls also remains on the list at 374 weeks and counting. A large variety of memoirs continue to be read and enjoyed.

In order to write a memoir, first the author must find the story in their situation (see Vivian Gornick's *The Situation and the Story*), and in order to do that, the author, who is also the narrator, in addition to a character in their own book, has to kind of climb out of the box of their own situation, and look back in to see the character of themselves participating in the story of their life.

This very act of climbing out of the box and looking back in to observe ourselves as a character in a story is a practice in mindfulness. It's as though we are observing our humanity—the experience of our very human lives—from our divinity, a kind of benevolent, compassionate, and empathetic observing awareness within us. That non-judgmental, observing awareness that we cultivate with mindfulness practices. This inner divinity is the same that exists in every sentient being and is a loving energy that connects us all. All of this provides insight into how we live as a spiritual being having a human experience, which includes both joy and pain. And as the author of memoir witnesses their humanity from their divinity, we as the reader are let into this mindfulness practice too.

In a good memoir, the author will make *meaning* from their experience; they'll search for a possible reason why events unfolded as they did, and they'll explore what they learned from their participation in the situation.

Historically, people have looked to religions to find meaning in our lives. But these days so many of us are looking for spiritual truths without the baggage that so often comes with organized religions. Perhaps this is part of the reason why memoir is so popular these days; no longer satisfied with religion and its crumbling patriarchal hierarchies, dogma and rules, the spiritual-but-not-religious crowd is looking to learn from the meaning people make from their experiences—as recorded in memoir.

Hence as we look for spiritual truths in places other than religion, we're learning from writers of memoir who find meaning in their stories that they convey to us through beautiful language and mastery of the craft of writing. In reading memoir, we experience the author performing an act of mindfulness and in doing so, as the reader, we participate in the practice of mindfulness as well.

Remaining Detached from Outcomes

If we're attached to a certain outcome, we will be elated if it happens, but crushed if it doesn't. If we practice being mindful of remaining detached from outcomes, we minimize our suffering. Easy to write about and a lifetime of mindfulness practice to master. But it does help alleviate suffering to at least be aware of this idea.

Remaining detached from the

fruits of our actions is one of the fundamental teachings in the ancient Hindu sacred text, *The Bhagavad Gita,* which we spent a year studying in interfaith seminary. I had never even heard of the *Gita* before, but so profound is the wisdom found in this epic poem from the world's oldest religion, I was inspired to read sections of this "Song of God" (as it is literally translated) in seven different translations, comparing them line by line. This concept of mindfully practicing remaining detached from outcomes is explored in depth.

As Rev. Stephanie Rutt writes in *An Ordinary Life Transformed: Lessons for Everyone from the Bhagavad Gita*: "True insight becomes ours when we keep our minds single-pointed and release attachment to the fruits of our actions . . . But such sweet surrender only occurs when we focus our intention on the *process*—not the *outcome*—of our actions and when we *need nothing* in return for our efforts."

This mini book on mindfulness prohibits the space needed to explore this idea in depth, but simply being introduced to this mindfulness concept will serve you well, and if you feel so inspired, I invite you to study the *Gita* in depth to excavate its spiritual wisdom in service to the evolution of your consciousness.

The many different translations available of the *Gita* offer subtle differences in meaning and some of the Sanskrit words have no exact translation. For example the word *dharma*, for which we do not even have an exact English equivalent, roughly translates to "the great work of your life" or to borrow the poet Mary Oliver's words: "What is it you will do with your one wild and precious life?"

"With mindfulness, we recognize the tension in our body, and we want very much to release it, but sometimes we can't. What we need is some insight. Insight is seeing what is there."

— Thich Nhat Hanh,
No Mud, No Lotus

Insight

We gain insight when we gain clarity.
By continually practicing mindfulness
exercises we develop the neural path-
ways in our brain to the point that we
more easily gain clarity and insight
around situations in our lives.

No Mud, No Lotus: We blossom like the lotus flower; *because of* our muck, not in spite of it

First we have to admit our muck (or negative seeds) to ourselves and own it. What do others find difficult about us? Being in a long-term relationship makes these things easy to identify—while our partners love us, they're also usually well acquainted with our muck.

Here are some examples of muck/opportunities for growth and blossoming:

Control Freak—we have an opportunity to learn the dance of will and surrender, and the joy and ecstasy that can be found in surrender.

Always Has to Be Right—we have an opportunity to learn that we are right for ourselves only. And rather than give advice, we can share the truth of our own experience while remaining detached from outcomes. This gives others the space to take what they need and to learn from our experience. It's no longer about our ego wanting control by having others take our advice.

Perfectionist—we have an opportunity to learn about the freedom, liberation, and immense enjoyment we can find with authenticity.

Sits in Judgment—we have an opportunity to learn to *observe* rather than to judge. Through simply *observing* without being *judgmental* and condemning something as worthless, we practice mindful acceptance of what is, which lessens our suffering in the long run.

Always the Victim—we have an opportunity to learn to re-frame our experience and own our own power. If we consider our soul designing this experience for us to learn certain lessons, we empower ourselves. As Viktor Frankl, the Holocaust survivor, Austrian neurologist, psychiatrist, and author of *Man's Search for Meaning* wrote: "We have absolutely no control over what happens to us in life but what we have paramount control over is how we respond to those events."

Argumentative and Short-tempered—we have an opportunity to learn to practice responding, not reacting.

Liar and a Cheat—we have an
opportunity to learn to observe how
cultivating these types of negative
seeds in ourselves only leads to greater
suffering in the long run, both for ourselves and for those we interact with.

Stubborn—we have an opportunity
to learn to practice flexibility and
mindful awareness of what the present moment requires of us. By practicing a mindful surrender to what is,
we learn to drop into the Flow of Life
and connect with Divine Love.

Procrastinator—we have an opportunity to learn that time is never wasted. It's all part of the learning experience.

When you've identified your own muck, first *know that you need it*. If you didn't have this very human muck you wouldn't be growing and blossoming from it. The universal story lies in our transformation from that muck. How do we blossom from our muck?

We become aware of it. The pain of self-awareness can be acute. To

know and own our very human
flaws and foibles is not as enjoyable
as knowing and owning our gifts.
But it is in the very act of identifying
and becoming aware of our muck
that we can identify our opportunity
for growth and transformation, and
lessen our suffering.

It made sense to me when I read
in Thich Nhat Hanh's book *No Mud,
No Lotus* that while Buddhism and
mindfulness look to alleviate suffering, even the Buddha suffered. The
Buddha was still human, and we are

still human, therefore we still suffer. What mindfulness helps us to do is to become better at suffering—it helps us handle our pain better. And to not be *attached* to our suffering.

We are reminded that we need our muck—our human suffering, pain, and difficulties, and like the lotus flower we blossom because of, not in spite of our muck. Our life's journey, our *dharma* (in the Hindu translation of the word: the great work of our life, or our "sacred duty") at an essential level, is about blossoming from our muck. As one translation of the ancient and sacred Hindu epic *The Bhagavad Gita* says: "Yoga is the practice of tolerating the consequence of being ourselves."

A Final Note

My husband and partner of twenty-four years has observed my own practice of mindfulness meditation over the years, and recently he said to me, "You know, mindfulness meditation is the gateway to spirituality."

May you enjoy further exploration into the wonderful Wisdom teachings of the ages.

— Rev. Camilla Sanderson

This book has been bound
using handcraft methods and
Smyth-sewn to ensure durability.

Illustrated by Kim Scafuro.

Designed by Ashley Haag.

Edited by Jennifer Leczkowski.

The text was set in Brandon
and Berkeley Oldstyle.